Sit & Solve

LOGIC
PUZZLES

MARK ZEGARELLI

Sterling Publishing Co., Inc. New York

Edited by Claire Bazinet

5 7 9 10 8 6 4

Published by Sterling Publishing Co., Inc.
387 Park Avenue South, New York, NY 10016
© 2003 by Mark Zegarelli
Distributed in Canada by Sterling Publishing
c/o Canadian Manda Group, One Atlantic Avenue, Suite 105
Toronto, Ontario, Canada M6K 3E7
Distributed in Great Britain by Chrysalis Books
64 Brewery Road, London N7 9NT, England
Distributed in Australia by Capricorn Link (Australia) Pty. Ltd.
P.O. Box 704, Windsor, NSW 2756, Australia

Printed in China
All rights reserved

Sterling ISBN 1-4027-0160-8

CONTENTS

PUZZLES

SHELF PUBLISHED

Minnie is a prolific author, having published three types of books. She keeps a copy of all of her published works on a set of three shelves (as shown below), with one type of books per shelf. Can you discover the type and number of books on each shelf?

top
middle
bottom

4

1. Minnie has written three more travel guides (which are on the top shelf) than mystery novels.

2. The cookbooks are on a shelf somewhere above the shelf that contains exactly seven books.

3. Minnie has written 25 books all together.

Answer on page 58.

KICKING THE HABITS

Over the last four years (1999–2002), Ezra has kicked four different habits, in each case using a different method (including psychotherapy). Can you link up each year with what Ezra quit and how he did it?

1. In 2000, Ezra quit smoking cigarettes.

2. He quit drinking coffee two years before he quit doing something with the help of a support group.

year	habit	method
1999		
2000		
2001		
2002		

3. Ezra used hypnosis to quit watching television.

4. He didn't quit desserts the year after he used a coach to kick a habit.

Answer on page 59.

5

PHILOSOPHERS AND STOOGES

On a snack break during a late-night study session, Anton and his two college roommates engaged in a passionate discussion about the relative merits of three existentialist philosophers while watching a Three Stooges marathon on TV. Can you discover each roommate's favorite philosopher and favorite stooge?

6

1. The student who prefers the writings of Albert Camus also most enjoys the antics of Larry.

2. Neil's favorite stooge isn't Moe.

3. The student who most respects Simone de Beauvoir's work doesn't favor Curly.

4. Fred's favorite existentialist is Jean-Paul Sartre.

Answer on page 60.

	Camus	de Beauvoir	Sartre	Moe	Larry	Curly
Anton						
Fred						
Neil						
Moe						
Larry						
Curly						

7

SUMMER EMPLOYMENT

During the summer, Jamie earned money by working for four neighbors, doing a different job for each. Discover who lives at each house, and which job Jamie did for each.

1. Zach hired Jamie to walk his dogs.
2. Either Angelica or Maurice lives at #141.
3. Raquel lives two houses east of the person who employed Jamie as a babysitter.
4. The neighbor who lives at #139 and the person who hired Jamie to do housecleaning are of opposite sexes.
5. The person who hired Jamie to do gardening doesn't live at #143.

West ← #137 #139 #141 #143 → East

Answer on page 61.

8

LIES AND WHISPERS

Two married couples work together in a library. The two technicians (audio/video and computer) always tell the truth while the two librarians (periodical and reference) always lie. Can you figure out each person's job?

Alan 1. Cori isn't the computer technician.

2. My wife isn't the reference librarian.

Bess 3. The technicians are both men.

Cori 4. Dirk is my husband.

Dirk 5. My wife is the periodical librarian.

name	job
Alan	
Bess	
Cori	
Dirk	

Answer on page 62.

BEAR WITH ME

Before bedtime last night, four of Veronica's relatives (including her brother) helped her act out the story of the Three Bears. Veronica played Goldilocks and each relative took the part of a different character (including Baby Bear). Can you discover how each person is related to Veronica and which part he took on?

1. Alex, who played Papa Bear, isn't Veronica's father.
2. Randall didn't play Mama Bear or the Big Bad Wolf.
3. Veronica's Uncle Glenn didn't play the Big Bad Wolf.
4. Neither Alex nor Larry is Veronica's grandfather.

Answer on page 63.

	brother	father	grandfather	uncle	Papa Bear	Mama Bear	Baby Bear	Big Bad Wolf
Alex								
Glenn								
Larry								
Randall								
Papa Bear								
Mama Bear								
Baby Bear								
Big Bad Wolf								

TIME TO TRAVEL

Since Eliza and Jim retired last year, they have visited each of their four children once, in each case in a different city (including Houston). Discover the month (including December) when they visited each person and the city where he or she now lives.

1. In January, Eliza and Jim visited Pamela.
2. Raymond lives in Las Vegas.
3. Neither Kenny nor Pamela lives in Tucson.
4. In October, Eliza and Jim didn't visit Kenny or Sylvia.
5. Pamela doesn't live in San Diego.
6. Eliza and Jim didn't visit Kenny in March.

12

Answer on page 64.

	Kenny	Pamela	Raymond	Sylvia	Houston	Las Vegas	San Diego	Tucson
Jan.								
Mar.								
Oct.								
Dec.								
Houston								
Las Vegas								
San Diego								
Tucson								

13

REASONABLE
SPECULATIONS—
VASTLY PLAUSIBLE

When Sean married Janay, the groom's four younger brothers all received invitations with an RSVP card enclosed. Each boy came to a different conclusion as to what those letters meant. Discover each brother's age (one is ten years old) and what he thought RSVP stood for.

1. Dale thought RSVP stands for "Remember–Send Verification Please."
2. Neither Jeff nor Linc thought that it stands for "Refreshments Served Very Promptly."
3. Alan isn't the twelve-year-old.
4. The boy who thought that the letters stand for "Rent Suit, Vest Preferred" (who isn't Linc) isn't the nine-year-old or the twelve-year-old.

5. The eleven-year-old thought that RSVP stands for "Regrets Severely Violently Punished."

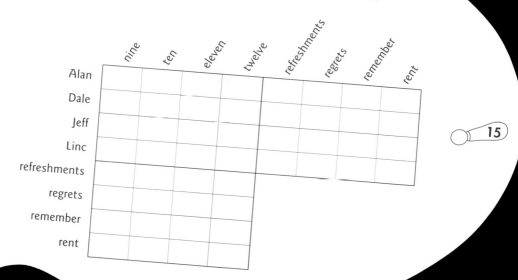

Answer on page 65.

MAY I CUT IN?

So many relatives wanted to dance with Janay at her wedding that her groom, Sean, barely got a turn. While the band played "Stardust," four relatives (including her father) took turns, each cutting in on the last. Figure out the order in which Janay danced with the four men and how each is related to her.

16

order	name	related
1st		
2st		
3rd		
4th		

1. Breece is Janay's cousin.

2. She danced with Elroy third.

3. Janay's grandfather didn't cut in on Darius.

4. Peter cut in on the man who had cut in on Janay's uncle.

Answer on page 66.

YOU GOTTA HAVE ART

In Art's house, four self-portraits are on display, each showing Art in a different location. See if you can discover what each painting depicts and the medium in which it is painted.

1. Painting #1 isn't in oils.

2. Painting #2 depicts Art either hang gliding or on his motorcycle.

3. The painting of Art next to a windmill is in either acrylics or tempera paints.

4. The painting of Art hang gliding and the work in tempera paints are in different rows.

5. The painting of Art surfing (which isn't in acrylics) is just above the watercolor.

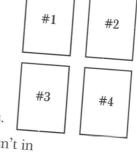

Answer on page 67.

BETTER
LATE

After over 50 years of marriage, Herman has never quite lived down the four anniversaries that he forgot—in each case, for a different reason. As a result, his wife, Darleen, received **very** impressive belated gifts those years. Can you match up each of these anniversaries with the reason that Herman forgot it and his gift?

1. Herman forgot his third anniversary because he was in the Army in Korea at the time.

2. For his ninth anniversary, he gave Darleen a trip to Bermuda.

3. For his 18th anniversary, Herman was either working late or traveling on business.

4. The year Herman got the date mixed up, he gave his wife an ermine coat.

5. When he forgot because he was traveling on business, he gave her either a ruby bracelet or a trip to Bermuda.

6. Herman gave Darleen a new Cadillac for either their 18th or their 34th anniversary.

anniversary	reason	gift
3rd		
9th		
18th		
34th		

19

Answer on page 68.

LIT UP

Members of the English literature department of the University of Avon are currently weighing the relative merits of four doctoral candidates (including Timothy). Find out where each candidate did his or her undergraduate work and his or her area of expertise.

1. The man from Duke isn't the expert on modernist novels.
2. Fiona didn't go to Temple.
3. The Stanford student isn't the expert on modernist novels or Victorian essays.
4. The student who went to Notre Dame and the expert on Shakespeare's historical plays are of opposite sexes.
5. George isn't the expert on Victorian essays.

6. The expert on romantic poetry (who didn't graduate from Duke or Stanford) isn't George or Rosa.

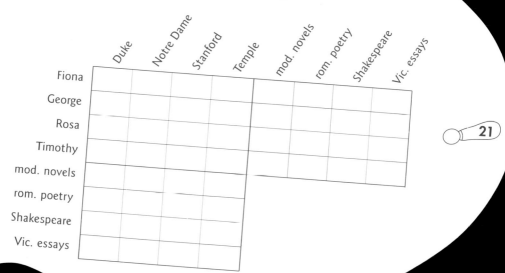

21

Answer on page 69

NESMA EXAM

As part of an entrance exam for NESMA–the National Extremely Smart Minds Association–four people (including Jenny and Alex) made the statements below. The married couple told the truth while the two single people lied. Can you identify each person and whether each is married or single?

22

Shorter man:

Taller man:

Shorter woman:

Taller woman:

1. I am not married to Rita.

2. I am Geoff.

3. Geoff is the shorter man.

4. The taller man is married to the shorter woman.

person	name	married/single
shorter man		
taller man		
shorter woman		
taller woman		

Answer on page 70.

KARAOKE QUEENS

The first five people to sing karaoke at Georgie's Bar last Wednesday night were all women (including Louise). Each woman sang a different song. Can you figure out the order in which the five women sang and each woman's selection?

1. Priscilla sang "Sweet Surrender."
2. Miriam sang second.
3. Naomi sang just after the woman who sang "Baby Love" and just before the woman who sang "Nothing Compares 2 U."
4. Olivia didn't sing just after the woman who sang "White Rabbit."
5. The fifth singer sang "I Will Survive."

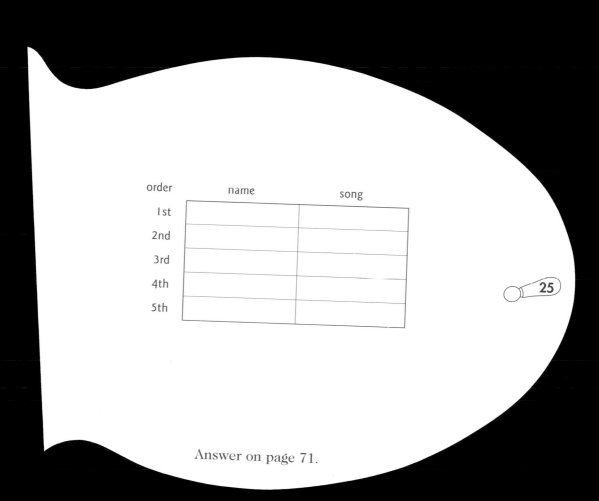

order	name	song
1st		
2nd		
3rd		
4th		
5th		

25

Answer on page 71.

HOME
IMPROVEMENT

Grover has spent the last five weekends working on home improvement projects. Can you figure out the order in which he worked on the projects and the friend (including Isaac) who helped him in each case?

1. Grover carpeted his basement the weekend after Jessica helped him.

2. He built a closet three weekends after Matthew helped him.

3. The fourth weekend, Grover either installed screen doors or refinished a wood floor.

4. Karl didn't help Grover to build a closet or install screen doors.

5. Either Laura or Matthew helped Grover to install light fixtures.

order	project	friend
1st		
2nd		
3rd		
4th		
5th		

Answer on pages 72–73.

27

REUNION
LUNCH

Gloria and three of her high school friends met for lunch the day before their 25th reunion. They sat at a square table, as shown here. Discover where each woman sat, the state where she currently lives, and what she ordered for lunch.

1. The woman who lives in Hawaii ordered chicken a la king.
2. Janey sat to the immediate right of the woman who lives in Idaho.
3. The woman who lives in Maine sat to the immediate left of the woman who ordered Hungarian goulash.
4. The woman who lives in Louisiana sat in seat #3.
5. Kelly didn't sit directly across from the woman who ordered the turkey platter.

6. Nisa, who didn't sit in seat #2, didn't order the broiled scrod or Hungarian goulash.
7. The women who live in Idaho and Maine sat directly cross from each other.

29

```
          #1

#4                    #2

          #3
```

Answer on page 74.

LOOKING FOR DIRECTION

As she exited the freeway, Mariah realized that she had left the directions to her new client's house in her office. She recalled that there were only three turns, in each case either right or left onto a different street, with a different landmark at each turn. She also recalled the random information below. Can you help her reconstruct the directions?

1. Mariah knows that the client lives on Mulberry Street, so this is her third turn.

2. She recalls that her first turn is at a firehouse.

3. At Guadalajara Way, Mariah must make a left.

4. Her first two turns are in the same direction.

5. The landmark at Avery Avenue is a supermarket.
6. Mariah must turn right at the church.

order	street	direction	landmark
I st			
2nd			
3rd			

31

Answer on page 75.

FAB FIVE

Five friends love the British TV sitcom "Absolutely Fabulous." Find out each woman's different favorite character (including Mother) and episode (including "Happy New Year" and "New Best Friend").

1. Noreen's favorite episode has the word "Happy" in its title.
2. "Fish Farm" isn't Kayla's or Leona's favorite.
3. The woman whose favorite character is Saffy isn't the one whose favorite episode is "Happy Birthday."
4. Bubble is either Leona's or Martina's favorite character.
5. Kayla (whose favorite character isn't Saffy) isn't the woman whose favorite episode is "Jealousy."
6. Jeanine's favorite character isn't Edina or Saffy.

7. Martina's favorite
episode has the word "New" in its title.
8. If Leona's favorite episode is "Jealousy,"
then her favorite character is Patsy.

	Bubble	Edina	Mother	Patsy	Saffy	Happy Birthday	Happy New Year	Jealousy	Fish Farm	New Best Friend
Jeanine										
Kayla										
Leona										
Martina										
Noreen										
Happy Birthday										
Happy New Year										
Jealousy										
Fish Farm										
New Best Friend										

Answer on page 76.

33

SUMMER READING

Miranda is a voracious reader of science fiction. During her summer vacation, she read a total of 15 books by five different writers. She also read a different number of books by each, in all cases completing all books by one author before beginning another author's work. Can you discover the order in which she read the books of the five authors and the number of books in each case?

34

1. Miranda read exactly two books by Kate Wilhelm, but didn't read them first.

2. She read an odd number of books by Doris Lessing.

3. She read Roger Zelazny fourth.

4. Miranda didn't read Stanislaw Lem first.

5. Ursula Le Guin is the third author that Miranda read after completing five books by another author.

6. Miranda read more books by women than by men.

order	author	# of books
1st		
2nd		
3rd		
4th		
5th		

35

Answer on page 77.

PHYSICIANS' FOURSOME

Four women, all of whom are physicians, play golf together every Sunday. Each player receives a handicap, a different number of strokes in each case, all numbers greater than zero. Can you match up each doctor with her specialty and handicap?

1. The dermatologist receives four more strokes than Dr. Radford.
2. Dr. Weiler gets a three-stroke handicap.
3. The anesthesiologist is either Dr. Radford or Dr. Ziales.
4. The ophthalmologist's handicap is an even number of strokes.
5. Dr. Ziales receives fewer than seven strokes.
6. Dr. Kandel receives fewer strokes than the podiatrist.

doctor	specialty	handicap

37

Answer on pages 78–79.

AFRICAN
ADVENTURES

Robert has been to Africa five times in five different years (1983, 1987, 1992, 1996, and 1999). In each case, he visited a different country with a different person. Figure out the year in which he visited each country and the person with whom he was traveling.

1. Robert visited Africa with a professor while he was in graduate school in 1992.
2. He and his son visited Nigeria together.
3. It was during an odd-numbered year that he traveled with a business colleague.
4. Robert traveled to Egypt during an even-numbered year.
5. He visited Kenya sometime before he visited Zaire.

38

6. Robert traveled with his best friend sometime in the 1980s.

7. He visited Morocco exactly four years after travelling with his wife.

year	country	companion
1983		
1987		
1992		
1996		
1999		

Answer on page 80.

DEAR SOPHIE

Sophie Stainwater writes a syndicated advice column called "Dear Sophie." At the end her last column, she briefly answered four questions asked in confidence, in one case responding "I wouldn't invite you either!" Match up each person's pseudonym (including Bewildered and Cautious) and city (including Augusta and Baltimore) with Sophie's response.

1. Sophie advised Disgruntled "Don't bet the farm on it!"

2. Adamant lives in Chicago.

3. Sophie told the person in Denver "She's the least of your worries!"

4. She replied "Take the money and run!" to a person whose pseudonym and home city have the same initial.

pseudonym	city	response

41

Answer on page 81.

HEAVY
BETTING

At a recent poker party, five friends sat at a circular table, as shown below. Heavy betting ensued when all five men held good cards during the same round. Can you figure out where each man sat and what hand he held during that round?

1. Eric sat in seat #1.

2. The man in seat #2 held either a straight or a flush.

3. The man in seat #3 wasn't Antony or Winston.

4. The man in seat #4 held two pairs.

5. Winston didn't sit to the immediate left of the man who held a straight.

6. Antony didn't sit next to the man who held three of a kind

7. Hank didn't hold a flush.

8. The man who held three of a kind sat next to the man who won with a full house; one of these two men is Gordon.

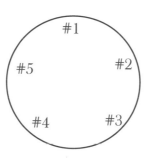

Answer on page 82.

43

SHOE
BUSINESS

Jerri repairs shoes for a local shoe store. Currently, she has four pairs of shoes, each from a different customer, all of which need some work done on them. Can you link up each person with the color and type of shoe that he or she owns and the type of repair that Jerri is doing?

1. The sandals have worn soles that need replacing.

2. Lenore owns the pumps, which aren't brown.

3. Dwayne owns the maroon shoes.

4. Maria's shoes have either a broken heel or a split instep.

5. A man owns the loafers.

6. The shoes that have a hole in the toe (which aren't Ralph's) aren't the pumps.

7. The boots are tan.

8. The black shoes don't have a split instep.

customer	color	shoe	repair

45

Answer on page 83.

SOLDIERS
AND SAILORS

At a family reunion, David met four distant cousins who
are in the U.S. military. All four wore dress uniforms, two
Army and two Navy. When David asked them their names and
where they are currently stationed, Terry and Tracy told the truth,
while Lee and Loren lied. This was especially confusing because
all four names can belong to either a man or a woman. Help
David figure out who is who and where each cousin is stationed
(including Florida).

46

Male soldier: _____

1. The male sailor is Terry.
2. Tracy isn't stationed in the Philippines.

Female soldier: _____

3. The female sailor isn't Terry.
4. Loren isn't stationed in England.

Male sailor:

Female sailor:

5. The male soldier is Lee.
6. The female sailor is Loren.
7. A sailor is stationed in Hawaii.
8. Tracy is stationed in the Philippines.

person	name	stationed
male soldier		
female soldier		
male sailor		
female sailor		

Answer on pages 84–85.

KNITTED OR CROCHETED?

Marion likes to knit and crochet, taking pleasure in creating hand-made gifts for her family. She gave each of her four most recent creations to a different person (including Frank). Discover the order in which Marion made these four items, the person to whom she gave each, and whether it was knitted or crocheted.

48

1. The two knitted items are the sweater and the first item that Marion made.

2. The two crocheted items are the baby blanket and the item that she gave to Dawn.

3. Marion gave the ski cap to a man.

4. The fourth item Marion made was a crocheted item that she gave to a woman.

5. She used different methods (i.e., knitting or crochet) to make the placemat set and the item that she gave to Elise.
6. She gave consecutive items to Dawn and George, in some order.

order	item	person	knitted/crocheted

Answer on pages 86–87.

LAWYERS'
ROUND TABLE

The five senior partners of Pinckney, Farkas, Delaney, Ewing, & Meems hold their regular Monday morning meetings at a round conference table. Can you discover where each person regularly sits and his or her specialty?

50

1. Ms. Pinckney sits in seat #1.

2. Ms. Delaney, who isn't the criminal defense lawyer, sits next to at least one man.

3. Ewing isn't the matrimonial lawyer.

4. The estate lawyer and the matrimonial lawyer are both men and sit next to each other.

5. The tax lawyer sits to the immediate right of a woman.

6. The criminal defense lawyer sits in seat #3
7. Farkas (who isn't the matrimonial lawyer) sits two seats
   to the right of the labor lawyer.

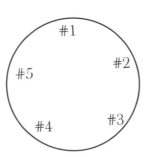

Answer on pages 88–89.

51

RECOVERING SOAP ADDICT

While recovering from a broken leg, Aaron got hooked on five different soap operas. Now, back to work, he secretly records them and catches up on his free evenings and weekends. Each story centers on a different woman in a different fictional setting. Can you link up each soap with its heroine and locale?

1. If Gabrielle is the heroine of "Hands of Time," then "Dream of Desire" isn't set in Stoneridge.
2. "Bridge Across the Night" takes place in either Barron County or Stoneridge.
3. "Dream of Desire" isn't set in Fallingsworth.
4. Rozlinn lives in Cole Canyon.
5. Neither Gabrielle nor Naomi lives in Stoneridge.

6. Zhora is the heroine of either "Eternal Flame" or "Dream of Desire."

7. "Hands of Time" takes place in either Stoneridge or Weston's Mill.

8. "Eternal Flame" is set in either Barron County or Cole Canyon.

9. Faith is the heroine of "The Searching Heart."

soap	heroine	setting

Answer on pages 90–91.

PREVARICATION PLACE

Soon after Kathleen moved into her new house on Prevarication Place, four neighbors dropped by to bring her housewarming gifts. As she got to know them, she realized that those who lived on the even side of the street always told the truth, while those on the odd side always lied. From their statements below, can you figure out each neighbor's house number and gift?

54

Arla   1. I live at either #55 or #66.
        2. The woman who lives at #75 brought the cake.

Bette   3. Cindi lives at either #32 or #75.
        4. Dina doesn't live at either #66 or #77.

Cindi   5. Bette and Dina live on the same side of the street.
        6. The woman who brought the salad doesn't
           live at #19 or #68.

7. If Arla brought the muffins, Dina doesn't live next door to me.

Dina
8. I live at either #66 or #77.
9. Either Arla or Bette brought the glazed ham.

neighbor	house #	gift

Answer on pages 92–93.

SCIENCE FRICTION

The science department at Rasputin High School is brimming with controversy. Each teacher is currently angry with a different teacher for a different reason (in one case, because another teacher told a joke at his or her expense). Discover each person's subject, the teacher with whom he or she is angry, and why.

1. No pair of teachers is angry at each other.

2. The chemistry teacher is angry with a man.

3. Mr. Hogarth is angry because another teacher commented on his weight.

4. The physics teacher is angry with Ms. Watson.

5. A woman is angry with another teacher who received a better class schedule.

6. A man is angry at Ms. Kessler, who teaches computers.

7. The person who is angry because another teacher scratched his or her car in the parking lot doesn't teach chemistry or physics.

8. Mr. Forbes doesn't teach biology.

teacher	subject	angry with	reason

Answer on pages 94–95.

ANSWERS

SHELF PUBLISHED

The top shelf contains travel guides (1). The cookbooks aren't on the bottom shelf (2), so they are on the middle shelf. By elimination, the bottom shelf contains mystery novels. There are seven of these (2), so there are ten travel guides (1). This accounts for 17 of the 25 books (3), so Minnie has written eight cookbooks.

58

top	travel guides	ten
middle	cookbooks	eight
bottom	mystery novels	seven

Puzzle on page 4.

KICKING
THE HABITS

In 2000, Ezra quit smoking cigarettes (1). He quit drinking coffee in 1999 and utilized a support group in 2001 (2). Ezra utilized hypnosis to quit watching television (3), so this was in 2002. By elimination, he quit eating desserts in 2001. He didn't use a coach in 2000 (4), so he used a psychotherapist. By elimination, he used a coach in 1999.

1999	coffee	coach
2000	cigarettes	psychotherapy
2001	desserts	support group
2002	television	hypnosis

Puzzle on page 5.

PHILOSOPHERS
AND STOOGES

One student prefers Camus and Larry (1). The student who likes Simone de Beauvoir doesn't favor Curly (3), so he likes Moe. By elimination, the student who likes Sartre also likes Curly. This student is Fred (4). Neil's favorite stooge isn't Moe (2), so he's Larry. By elimination, Anton's favorite stooge is Moe.

60

Anton	de Beauvoir	Moe
Fred	Sartre	Curly
Neil	Camus	Larry

Puzzle on pages 6–7.

SUMMER EMPLOYMENT

Either Angelica or Maurice lives at #141 (2). Raquel lives at #143 and the person at #139 employed Jamie as a babysitter (3). Zach hired Jamie to walk his dogs (1), so he lives at #137. Raquel, at 143, didn't hire Jamie to do gardening (5), so the person at #141 hired her to do gardening. By elimination, Raquel hired Jamie to do housecleaning. Thus, a man lives at #139 (4), so he's Maurice. By elimination, Angelica lives at #141.

#137	Zach	walking dogs
#139	Maurice	babysitting
#141	Angelica	gardening
#143	Raquel	housecleaning

Puzzle on page 8.

61

LIES AND WHISPERS

If Bess told the truth, then she would be a technician (intro), which is a contradiction (3). Thus, Bess lied, so she's a librarian (intro). The technicians aren't both men (3), so Cori is a technician. Thus, Cori told the truth (intro), so she's Dirk's wife (4). By elimination, Alan is married to Bess. Statement 5 is false, so Dirk lied, so he's a librarian (intro). By elimination, Alan is a technician, so he told the truth (intro). Cori isn't the computer technician (1), so she's the audio/video technician. By elimination, Alan is the computer technician. His wife, Bess, isn't the reference librarian (2), so Dirk is (see above). By elimination, Bess is the periodical librarian.

Alan	computer technician
Bess	periodical librarian
Cori	audio/video technician
Dirk	reference librarian

Puzzle on page 9.

62

BEAR
WITH ME

Alex played Papa Bear (1). Randall didn't play Mama Bear or the Big Bad Wolf (2), so he played Baby Bear. Glenn didn't play the Big Bad Wolf (3), so Larry did. By elimination, Glenn played Mama Bear. He's Veronica's uncle (3). Neither Alex nor Larry is Veronica's grandfather (4), so Randall is. Alex isn't her father (1), so he's her brother. By elimination, Larry is her father.

Alex	brother	Papa Bear
Glenn	uncle	Mama Bear
Larry	father	Big Bad Wolf
Randall	grandfather	Baby Bear

Puzzle on pages 10–11.

TIME TO
TRAVEL

In January, Eliza and Jim visited Pamela (1). In October,
they didn't visit Kenny or Sylvia (4), so they visited Raymond.
They didn't visit Kenny in March (6), so they visited him in
December. By elimination, they visited Sylvia in March. Raymond
lives in Las Vegas (2). Neither Kenny nor Pamela lives in Tucson
(3), so Sylvia does. Pamela doesn't live in San Diego (5), so
Kenny does. By elimination, Sylvia lives in Houston.

64

January	Pamela	Houston
March	Sylvia	Tucson
October	Raymond	Las Vegas
December	Kenny	San Diego

Puzzle on pages 12–13.

REASONABLE SPECULATIONS—VASTLY PLAUSIBLE

Dale thought RSVP stands for "Remember–Send Verification Please" (1). Neither Jeff nor Linc thought that the letters stand for "Refreshments Served Very Promptly" (2), so Alan did. Linc didn't think that they stand for "Rent Suit, Vest Preferred" (4), so Jeff did. By elimination, Linc thought that they stand for "Regrets Severely Violently Punished," so he's eleven (5). Jeff isn't nine or twelve (4), so he's ten. Alan isn't twelve years old (3), so he's nine. By elimination, Dale is twelve.

Alan	nine	"Refreshments Served Very Promptly."
Dale	twelve	"Remember–Send Verification Please"
Jeff	ten	"Rent Suit, Vest Preferred"
Linc	eleven	"Regrets Severely Violently Punished"

Puzzle on pages 14–15.

MAY I
CUT IN?

Elroy danced with Janay third (2). Peter was the second man to dance with Janay's after her uncle (4), so Peter was fourth and her uncle was second. Breece is Janay's cousin (1), so he danced with her first. By elimination, Darius danced with her second. Elroy cut in on Darius (see above), so he isn't Janay's grandfather (3), so he's her father. By elimination, Peter is her grandfather.

66

1st	Breece	cousin
2nd	Darius	uncle
3rd	Elroy	father
4th	Peter	grandfather

Puzzle on page 16.

YOU GOTTA
HAVE ART

Painting #2 depicts Art either hang gliding or on his motorcycle. (2). The painting of Art surfing is #1 and the watercolor is #3 (5). The painting of Art next to a windmill is in either acrylics or tempera paints (3), so it's #4. The oil painting isn't painting #1 (1), so it's #2. The acrylic doesn't depict Art surfing (5), so it shows him next to a windmill. By elimination, the painting of Art surfing is in temperas. Painting #3 depicts Art hang gliding (4). By elimination, painting #2 depicts Art on his motorcycle.

#1	surfing	temperas
#2	motorcycle	oils
#3	hang gliding	watercolors
#4	windmill	acrylics

Puzzle on page 17.

BETTER
LATE

Herman forgot his 3rd anniversary because he was in Korea at the time (1). For the 9th, he gave Darleen a trip to Bermuda (2). For the 18th, Herman was either working late or traveling on business (3). When Herman got the date mixed up, he gave Darleen an ermine coat (4), so this was for the 34th. Thus, he gave her a new Cadillac for the 18th (6). By elimination, he gave her a ruby bracelet for the 3rd. When he was traveling on business, he gave her a trip to Bermuda (5). By elimination, when he was working late he gave her a new Cadillac.

3rd	in Korea	ruby bracelet
9th	traveling on business	trip to Bermuda
18th	working late	new Cadillac
34th	mixed-up date	ermine coat

Puzzle on pages 18–19.

68

LIT UP

The Stanford student isn't the expert on modernist novels or Victorian essays (3), or romantic poetry (6), so he or she is the expert on Shakespeare's historical plays. The man from Duke isn't the expert on modernist novels (1) or romantic poetry (6), so he's the expert on Victorian essays. He isn't George (5), so he's Timothy. The expert on romantic poetry isn't George or Rosa (6), so she's Fiona. She didn't go to Temple (2), so she went to Notre Dame. Thus, the Shakespeare expert is a man (4), so he's George. By elimination, Rosa is the expert on modernist novels, and attended Temple.

69

Fiona	Notre Dame	romantic poetry
George	Stanford	Shakespeare's historicals
Timothy	Duke	Victorian essays
Rosa	Temple	modernist novels

Puzzle on pages 20–21.

NESMA
EXAM

The taller man and shorter woman made statements that contradict each other, so they aren't married to each other (intro). Thus, the taller woman lied (4), so she's single (intro). By elimination, the shorter woman is married, so she told the truth (intro). Thus, Geoff is the shorter man (3). By elimination, Alex is the taller man. He lied (2), so he's single. By elimination, the shorter man is married to the shorter woman. He told the truth (intro), so he isn't married to Rita (1), so he's married to Jenny. Thus, Jenny is the shorter woman. By elimination, Rita is the taller woman.

70

Puzzle on pages 22–23.

KARAOKE
QUEENS

Miriam sang second (2). The fifth singer sang "I Will Survive" (5). Naomi didn't sing first or fifth (3). If she had sung fourth, the woman who sang "Nothing Compares 2 U" would have sung fifth (3), a contradiction. Thus, Naomi sang third. Miriam, who sang second (see above), sang "Baby Love" and the fourth singer sang "Nothing Compares 2 U" (3). Priscilla sang "Sweet Surrender" (1), so she sang first. By elimination, Naomi sang "White Rabbit." She sang third (see above), so Olivia didn't sing fourth (4), so Olivia sang fifth. By elimination, Louise sang fourth.

71

1st	Priscilla	"Sweet Surrender"
2nd	Miriam	"Baby Love"
3rd	Naomi	"White Rabbit"
4th	Louise	"Nothing Compares 2 U"
5th	Olivia	"I Will Survive"

Puzzle on pages 24–25.

HOME
IMPROVEMENT

The 4th weekend, Grover either installed screen doors or refinished a wood floor (3). He didn't build a closet the 1st, 2nd, or 3rd weekend (2), so he built a closet the 5th weekend and Matthew helped him the 2nd weekend (2). He didn't carpet the basement the 1st or 3rd weekend (1), so he carpeted the basement the 2nd weekend and Jessica helped him the 1st weekend (1). Thus, Matthew helped Grover carpet the basement (see above). Laura helped Grover to install light fixtures (5), so this was the 3rd weekend (see above). Karl didn't help Grover to build a closet (4), so Isaac did. By elimination, Karl helped Grover the 4th week. He didn't help install the screen doors (4), so Jessica did. By elimination, Karl helped refinish the wood floor.

72

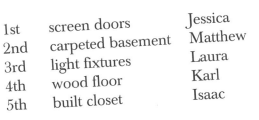

1st	screen doors	Jessica
2nd	carpeted basement	Matthew
3rd	light fixtures	Laura
4th	wood floor	Karl
5th	built closet	Isaac

Puzzle on pages 26–27.

REUNION
LUNCH

The woman who lives in Louisiana sat in seat #3 (4). The woman directly across from her, in #1, isn't from Idaho or Maine (7), so she's from Hawaii. She ordered chicken a la king (1). The woman who lives in Maine sat in #4 and the woman who ordered Hungarian goulash sat in #3 (3). By elimination, the woman who lives in Idaho sat in #2. Janey sat in #1 (2). Nisa didn't sit in #2 or #3 (6), so she sat in #4. She didn't order broiled scrod (6), so the woman in #2 ordered it. By elimination, Nisa ordered a turkey platter. Kelly didn't sit in #2 (5), so she sat in #3. By elimination, Gloria sat in #2.

#1 Janey   Hawaii   chicken a la king
#2 Gloria   Idaho   broiled scrod
#3 Kelly   Louisiana Hungarian goulash
#4 Nisa   Maine   turkey platter

Puzzle on pages 28–29.

74

LOOKING FOR
DIRECTION

The third turn is onto Mulberry Street (1). The first turn is
at a firehouse (2). The landmark at Avery Avenue is a supermarket (5), so this is the second turn. By elimination, the first turn
is onto Guadalajara Way, so this is a left turn (3). The second turn
is also left (4). By elimination, the third turn is at a church, so
this is right (6).

1st	Guadalajara Way	left	firehouse
2nd	Avery Avenue	left	supermarket
3rd	Mulberry Street	right	church

Puzzle on pages 30–31.

FAB FIVE

"Fish Farm" isn't Noreen's favorite (1), or Kayla's or Leona's (2), or Martina's (7), so it's Jeanine's. "Jealousy" isn't Noreen's favorite (1), or Kayla's (5), or Martina's (7), so it's Leona's. Her favorite character is Patsy (8). Bubble is Martina's favorite character (4). Jeanine's favorite character isn't Edina or Saffy (9), so it's Mother. Kayla's favorite char-acter isn't Saffy (5), so it's Edina. By elimination, Noreen's favorite is Saffy. Her favorite episode isn't "Happy Birthday" (3), so it's "Happy New Year" (1). Martina's favorite episode is "New Best Friend" (7). By elimination, Kayla's is "Happy Birthday."

Jeanine	Mother	"Fish Farm"
Kayla	Edina	"Happy Birthday"
Leona	Patsy	"Jealousy"
Martina	Bubble	"New Best Friend"
Noreen	Saffy	"Happy New Year"

76

Puzzle on pages 32–33.

SUMMER READING

Miranda read Roger Zelazny fourth (3). She didn't read Ursula Le Guin first, second, or third (5), so she read Le Guin fifth and read five books by the second author (5). She read two books by Kate Wilhelm, but not first (1), so third. She didn't read Stanislaw Lem first (4), so she read him second. By elimination, she read Doris Lessing first. She read at least eight books by women (6), so she read fewer than three books by Roger Zelazny, so she read one book by him. She read three books by Doris Lessing (2). By elimination, she read four books by Ursula Le Guin.

77

1st	Doris Lessing	three
2nd	Stanislaw Lem	five
3rd	Kate Wilhelm	two
4th	Roger Zelazny	one
5th	Ursula Le Guin	four

Puzzle on page 34.

PHYSICIANS'
FOURSOME

The anesthesiologist is either Dr. Radford or Dr. Ziales (3).
The ophthalmologist's handicap is an even number of strokes (4).
Dr. Weiler gets a three-stroke handicap (2), so she isn't the dermatologist (1), so Dr. Weiler is the podiatrist. The dermatologist receives
more than four strokes (1). Dr. Kandel gets one or two strokes
(6), so she's isn't the dermatologist (see above). Thus, she's the
ophthal-mologist, so she receives two strokes (4). Dr. Radford
isn't the dermatologist (1), so she's the anesthesiologist. By elimination, Dr. Ziales is the dermatologist. She receives more than four
strokes (1) and fewer than seven (5), so she receives either five or
six strokes. Thus, Dr. Radford receives either one or two (1).
She doesn't receive two strokes, because Dr. Kandel
does (intro), so Dr. Radford receives one
stroke and Dr. Ziales receives five (1).

Dr. Kandel   ophthalmologist   two
Dr. Radford   anesthesiologist   one
Dr. Weiler   podiatrist   three
Dr. Ziales   dermatologist   five

79

Puzzle on pages 36–37.

AFRICAN
ADVENTURES

Robert visited Africa with a professor in 1992 (1). He visited Morocco in 1987 and traveled with his wife in 1983 (7). He traveled with his best friend in 1987 (6). He traveled with a business colleague in 1999 (3). By elimination, he traveled with his son in 1996, so this trip was to Nigeria (2). He traveled to Egypt in 1992 (4). He visited Kenya in 1983 and Zaire in 1999 (5).

1983	Kenya	wife
1987	Morocco	best friend
1992	Egypt	professor
1996	Nigeria	son
1999	Zaire	business colleague

Puzzle on pages 38–39.

DEAR SOPHIE

Sophie advised Disgruntled "Don't bet the farm on it!" (1). Adamant lives in Chicago (2). Sophie told the person in Denver "She's the least of your worries!" (3). She replied "Take the money and run!" to Bewildered in Baltimore (4). By elimination, Cautious lives in Denver, Disgruntled lives in Augusta, and Sophie replied "I wouldn't invite you either!" to Adamant in Chicago.   81

Adamant	Chicago	"I wouldn't invite you either!"
Bewildered	Baltimore	"Take the money and run!"
Cautious	Denver	"She's the least of your worries!"
Disgruntled	Augusta	"Don't bet the farm on it!"

Puzzle on pages 40–41.

HEAVY BETTING

The man in seat #2 held either a straight or a flush (2).
The man in seat #4 held two pairs (4). Thus, the men who
held three of a kind and a full house sat, in some order, in seats
#1 and #5 (8). Eric sat in #1 (1), so Gordon sat in #5 (8). The man
in seat #3 wasn't Antony or Winston (3), so he was Hank. He didn't
hold a flush (7), so the man in seat #2 held a flush. By
elimination, Hank, in #3 (see above), held a straight, so the
man to his immediate left, in #4, was not Winston (5), so
Winston sat in seat #2. By elimination, Antony sat in #4. Gordon,
in #5 (see above), didn't hold three of a kind (6), so Eric did. By
elimination, Gordon won the round with a full house.

82

#1 Eric three of a kind		#3 Hank straight
#2 Winston flush		#4 Antony two pairs
	#5 Gordon full house	

Puzzle on pages 42–43.

SHOE BUSINESS

The sandals have worn soles (1). Lenore owns the pumps (2). A man owns the loafers (5). The boots are tan (7). This accounts for the four pairs of shoes. Maria's shoes have either a broken heel or a split instep (4), so they are the tan boots (see above). The pumps don't have a hole in the toe (6), so the loafers do (see above). They don't belong to Ralph (6), so Ralph owns the sandals. By elimination, Dwayne owns the loafers. These are maroon (3). Lenore's pumps aren't brown (2), so Ralph's sandals are brown. By elimination, Lenore's pumps are black. They don't have the split instep (8), so they have the broken heel. By elimination, Maria's shoes have the split instep.

Dwayne	maroon loafers	hole in toe
Lenore	black pumps	broken heel
Maria	tan boots	split instep
Ralph	brown sandals	worn soles

Puzzle on pages 44–45.

SOLDIERS
AND SAILORS

The male soldier and the female sailor made statements
that are contradictory (2 & 8), so one of them told the truth
and the other lied. Thus, their names begin with different letters
(intro), so statements 5 and 6 aren't both true. Thus, the male sailor
lied, so he's either Lee or Loren (intro). Statement 1 is false, so
the male soldier lied. He can't be Lee (since statement 5 is a
lie), so he's Loren, and by elimination, the male sailor is Lee.
By elimination, the two women told the truth and are named Terry
and Tracy (intro). The female sailor isn't Terry (3), so the female
soldier is Terry, and by elimination, the female sailor is Tracy.
She's stationed in the Philippines (8). A sailor is stationed in
Hawaii (7), so he's the male sailor. Loren isn't stationed
in England (4), so he's stationed in Florida. By
elimination, Terry is stationed in
England.

Male soldier	Loren	Florida
Female soldier	Terry	England
Male sailor	Lee	Hawaii
Female sailor	Tracy	Philippines

85

Puzzle on pages 46–47.

KNITTED OR CROCHETED?

The two knitted items are the sweater and the first item
that Marion made (1). The two crocheted items are the baby
blanket and the item that she gave to Dawn (2). This accounts for
all four items. Marion gave the ski cap to a man (3), so, of the four
items that we have enumerated, the ski cap is the first item
that Marion made. By elimination, she gave the placemat set
to Dawn. This is crochetted (see above), so the item that she
gave to Elise is knitted(5), so this is the sweater. By elimination, she
gave the baby blanket to a man. Thus, the placemat set is the only
crocheted item that Marion gave to a woman, so she made this
item fourth (4). She gave the third item to George (6), so
this is the baby blanket (see above). By elimination,
she made the sweater second and gave
the ski cap to Frank.

86

1st	ski cap	Frank	knitted
2nd	sweater	Elise	knitted
3rd	baby blanket	George	crocheted
4th	placemat set	Dawn	crocheted

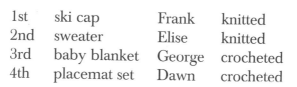

87

Puzzle on pages 48–49.

LAWYERS'
ROUND TABLE

Ms. Pinckney sits in seat #1 (1). The criminal defense lawyer sits in seat #3 (6). The estate lawyer and the matrimonial lawyer are both men and sit next to each other (4), so they sit, in some order, in seats #4 and #5. Ms. Delaney isn't the criminal defense lawyer (2), so she sits in seat #2. Thus, the criminal defense lawyer, in seat #3 (see above), is a man (2). Ms. Delaney isn't the tax lawyer (5), so Ms. Pinckney is. By elimination, Ms. Delaney is the labor lawyer. She sits in seat #2 (see above), so Farkas sits in seat #5 (7). He isn't the matrimonial lawyer (7), so he's the estate lawyer. By elimination, the matrimonial lawyer sits in seat #4. He isn't Ewing (3), so he's Meems. By elimination, Ewing sits in seat #3.

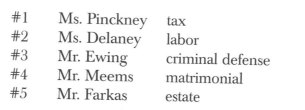

#1	Ms. Pinckney	tax
#2	Ms. Delaney	labor
#3	Mr. Ewing	criminal defense
#4	Mr. Meems	matrimonial
#5	Mr. Farkas	estate

Puzzle on pages 50–51.

RECOVERING
SOAP ADDICT

"Bridge Across the Night" takes place in either Barron
County or Stoneridge (2). Rozlinn lives in Cole Canyon (4).
Zhora is the heroine of either "Eternal Flame" or "Dream of
Desire" (6). "Hands of Time" takes place in either Stoneridge or
Weston's Mill (7). Faith is the heroine of "The Searching Heart"
(9). This accounts for the five soaps. By elimination, Gabrielle
and Naomi are the heroines of, in some order, "Bridge Across
the Night" and "Hands of Time." Thus, neither of these soaps is set
in Stoneridge (5), so "Bridge Across the Night" is set in Barron
County (2) and "Hands of Time" is set in Weston's Mill (7).
"Eternal Flame" is set in Cole Canyon (8), so the heroine
of this show is Rozlinn (see above). By elimination,
Zhora is the heroine of "Dream of Desire."

This show isn't set in Fallingsworth (3), so "The Searching Heart" is set there. By elimination, "Dream of Desire" is set in Stoneridge. Thus, Gabrielle isn't the heroine of "Hands of Time" (1), so Naomi is. By elimination, Gabrielle is the heroine of "Bridge Across the Night."

"Bridge Across the Night"	Gabrielle	Barron County
"Hands of Time"	Naomi	Weston's Mill
"The Searching Heart"	Faith	Fallingsworth
"Eternal Flame"	Rozlinn	Cole Canyon
"Dream of Desire"	Zhora	Stoneridge

91

Puzzle on pages 52–53.

PREVARICATION PLACE

Statements 4 and 8 are contradictory, so Bette and Dina live on opposite sides of the street (intro). Thus, statement 5 is false, so Cindi lives on the odd side (intro). By elimination, Arla lives on the even side. She tells the truth (intro), so she lives at #66 (1). If Dina lived on the even side, statement 8 would be true (intro), so she would live at #66, which is a contradiction. Thus, Dina lives on the odd side and, by elimination, Bette lives on the even side. Cindi lives at #75 (3), so she brought the cake (2). Neither Arla nor Bette brought the glazed ham (9), so Dina did. Bette lives at #68 and brought the salad (6). By elimination, Arla brought the muffins. Dina lives next door to Cindi (7). Since Arla and Bette live at #66 and #68, neighboring houses are two numbers apart. Thus, since Dina doesn't live at #77 (4), she lives at #73.

Arla	#66	muffins
Bette	#68	salad
Cindi	#75	cake
Dina	#73	glazed ham

93

Puzzle on pages 64–65.

SCIENCE
FRICTION

The physics teacher is angry with Ms. Watson (4). Ms. Watson is angry with a third person (1). This third person is angry with a fourth person, who in turn is angry with the physics teacher (1). This accounts for all four people. A man is angry with Ms. Kessler, who teaches computers (6), so this man is the third person enumerated above and Ms. Kessler is the fourth (see above). The chemistry teacher is angry with a man (2), so Ms. Watson teaches chemistry. By elimination, the biology teacher is angry with Ms. Kessler. Mr. Forbes doesn't teach biology (8), so he teaches physics. By elimination, Mr. Hogarth teaches biology. He is angry because Ms. Kessler commented on his weight (3). The person who is angry because another teacher scratched his or her car doesn't teach chemistry or physics (7), so she's Ms. Kessler, who teaches computers. Ms. Watson is angry that Mr. Hogarth received a better class schedule (5). By elimination, Mr. Forbes is angry that Ms. Watson told a joke at his expense.

teacher	subject	angry with	reason
Mr. Forbes	physics	Ms. Watson	joke
Mr. Hogarth	biology	Ms. Kessler	weight
Ms. Kessler	computers	Mr. Forbes	car
Ms. Watson	chemistry	Mr. Hogarth	schedule

Puzzle on pages 56–57.

INDEX